1100
DECORATIVE FRENCH
IRONWORK DESIGNS

1100 DECORATIVE FRENCH IRONWORK DESIGNS

Denonvilliers Company

DOVER PUBLICATIONS, INC.
Mineola, New York

Publisher's Note

The vast array of graceful, functional designs featured in a catalog of the L. Denonvilliers firm, manufacturers of wrought iron and cast iron, can serve as a source of ideas for modern architects, metalcrafters, building contractors, interior decorators, and owners of both urban and rural homes. The ironworks, which maintained its showrooms in Paris during the latter part of the 19th century (taking over the Auguste Godard firm), operated foundries in the Haute-Marne region.

The flourishing trade in wrought iron and cast iron for interior and exterior decorative and utilitarian purposes built on a long European tradition that had been transplanted to Latin America and the southern United States, but was amplified after 1850 by the trend, in western Europe and the United States, for using iron structural elements in architecture. The impact created by the impressive and thoroughly modern glass-and-iron Crystal Palace (designed by Sir Joseph Paxton and built for the Great Exhibition of London, held in 1851), and by the development of the Cast-Iron District in New York City (on and around Sixth Avenue between West 23rd and West 14th streets) gave impetus to the increasing use of wrought iron designs in homes and public buildings. Although iron "skeletons" represented modernity in the construction of buildings, enabling taller structures to be erected

than ever before, wrought-iron creations used as nonarchitectural decorative elements usually relied heavily on classical and medieval allusions to mythology, legends, religion, history, and literature, as well as traditional botanical forms, such as the palm leaf and the pineapple.

Among the wide range of designs offered by the L. Denonvilliers firm were wrought-iron grillwork for indoor and outdoor use on windows and doors; elements of fencing, railings, and gates that could be joined in customized combinations to create a myriad of patterns and motifs; banisters, newel posts, and decorations for stairways; small hardware for doors; gargoyles and heads; frames and bases for indoor and garden furniture such as tables, chairs, and benches; small items for the home, including clotheshorses, hat hooks, umbrella stands, fireplace racks, and candlesticks. In addition, the firm produced architectural columns; household sinks and pipes as well as decorative fountains and spigots; utility cast-iron and forged items, such as frames for bulletin boards, siphons, roasting ovens and pans, funnels, pulleys, base plates, door peepholes, and street drains, suitable for use in public buildings, in restaurants and kitchens, and on sidewalks. Religious items (statues and crosses), and burial-related creations (from small ornaments to monuments and tomb enclosures) completed the company's offerings.

Bibliographical Note

This Dover edition, first published in 2001, is a republication of 1,100 designs from *Fontes de fer de toutes espèces,* a catalog published by the L. Denonvilliers firm, Paris, circa 1900. A new Publisher's Note has been prepared for the Dover edition.

DOVER *Pictorial Archive* SERIES

Library of Congress Cataloging-in-Publication Data

1100 decorative French ironwork designs.
     p. cm.
    Reprint. Originally published: Paris : Denonvilliers firm, 1900?.
    ISBN 0-486-41223-7 (pbk.)
    1. Ironwork—France—History—19th century—Themes, motives—Catalogs. I. Title: One thousand one hundred decorative French ironwork designs. II. Title: One thousand and one hundred decorative French ironwork designs.

NK8249.A1 A16 2001
739.4'744—dc21
                                                      00-058962

Manufactured in the United States of America
Dover Publications, Inc., 31 East 2nd Street, Mineola, N.Y. 11501

Plate 1. Windowsills

Plate 2. Windowsills

Plate 3. Windowsills

Plate 4. Window Balconies

Plate 5. Window Balconies

Plate 6. Window Balconies

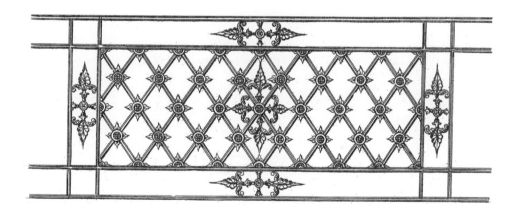

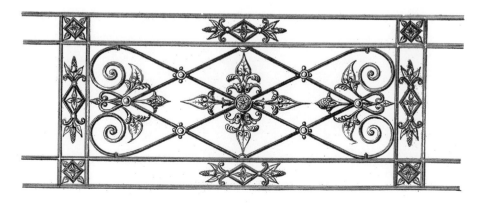

Plate 7. Window Balconies

Plate 8. Window Balconies

Plate 9. Window Balconies

Plate 10. Window Balconies

Plate 11. Window Balconies

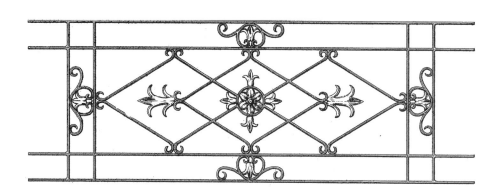

Plate 12. Window Balconies

Plate 13. Window Balconies

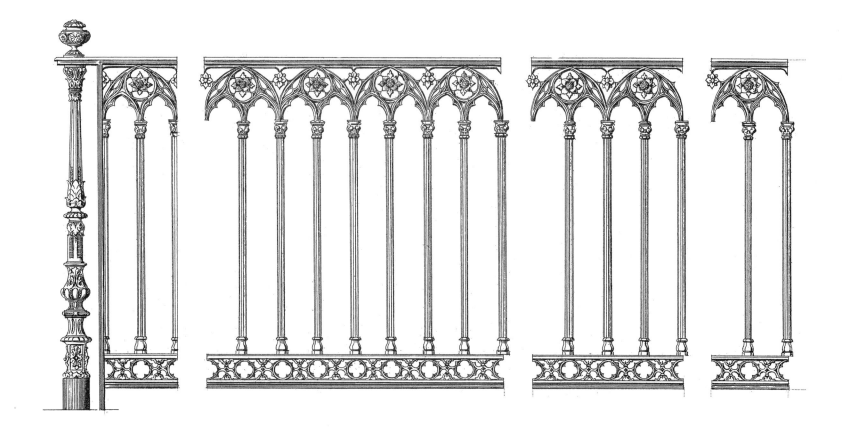

Plate 14. Large Balconies and Railings

Plate 15. Large Balconies and Railings

Plate 16. Large Balconies and Railings

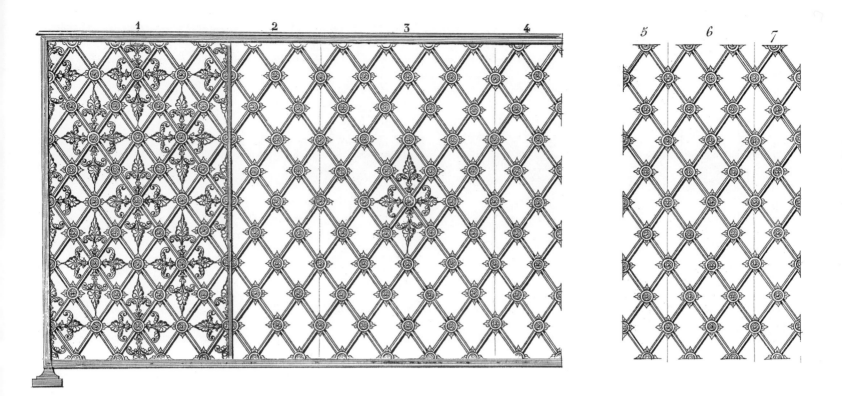

Plate 17. Large Balconies and Railings

Plate 18. Large Balconies and Railings

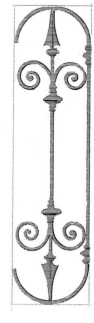

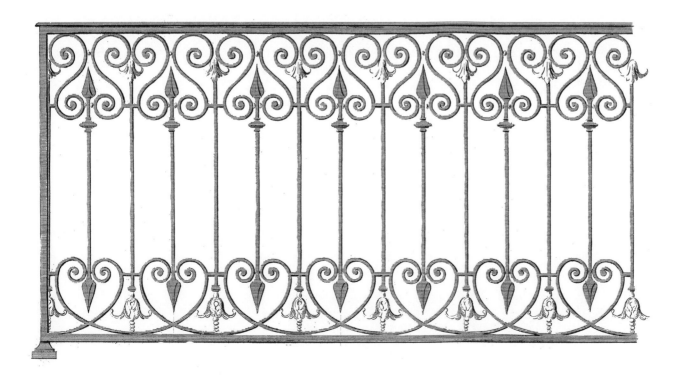
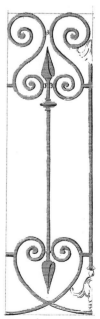

Plate 19. Large Balconies and Railings

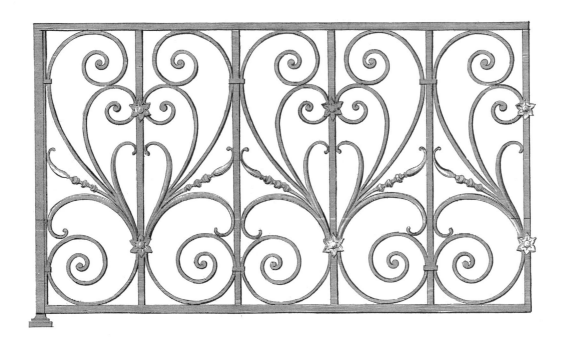

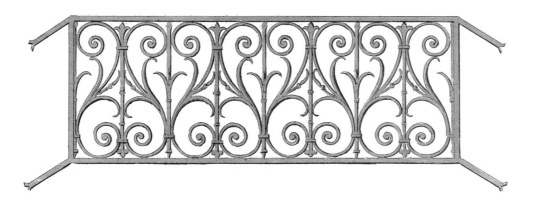

Plate 20. Large Balconies and Railings

Plate 21. Large Balconies and Railings

Plate 22. Large Balconies and Railings

Plate 23. Large Balconies and Railings

Plate 24. Large Balconies and Railings

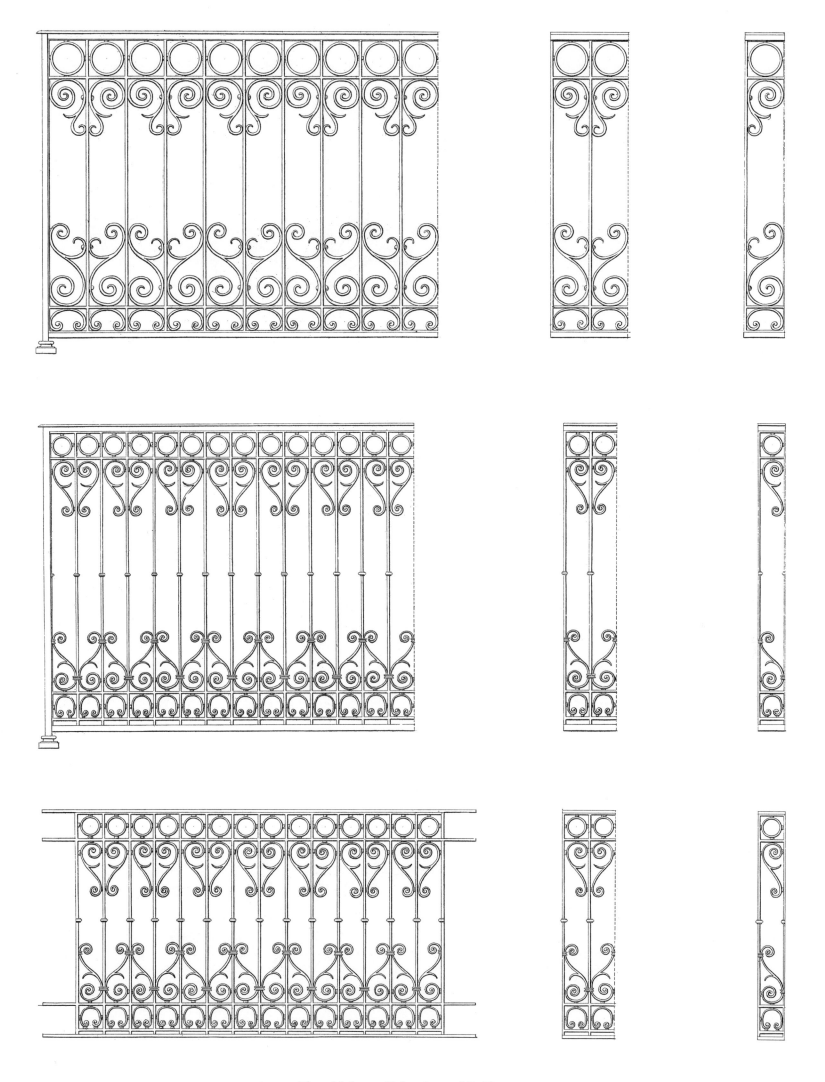

Plate 25. Large Balconies and Railings

Plate 26. Large Balconies and Railings

Plate 27. Large Balconies and Railings

Plate 28. Large Balconies and Railings

Plate 29. Large Balconies and Railings

Plate 30. Large Balconies and Railings

Plate 31. Large Balconies and Railings

Plate 32. Large Balconies and Railings

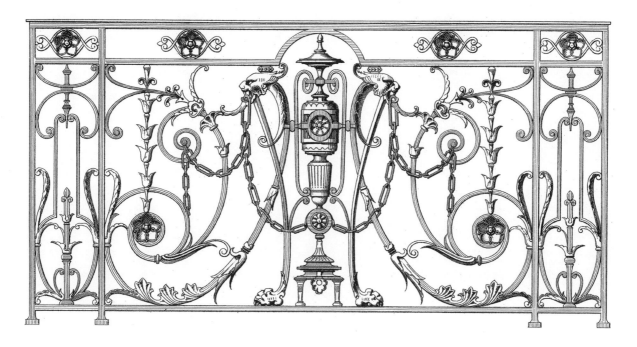

Plate 33. Large Balconies and Railings

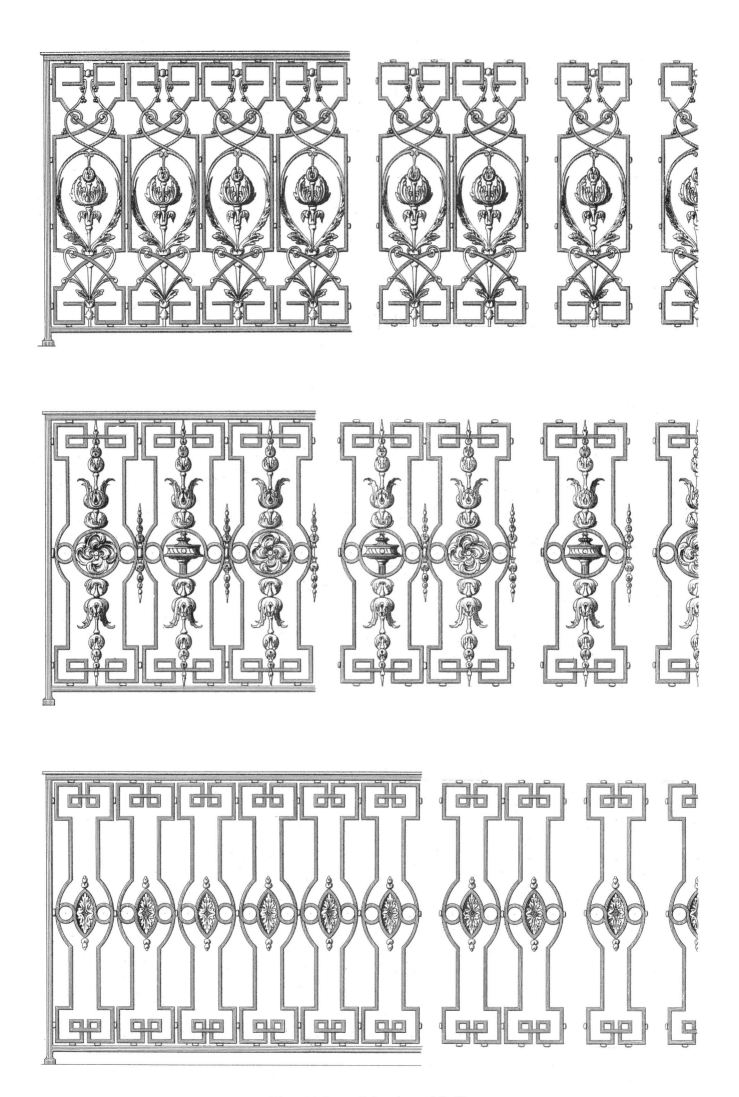

Plate 34. Large Balconies and Railings

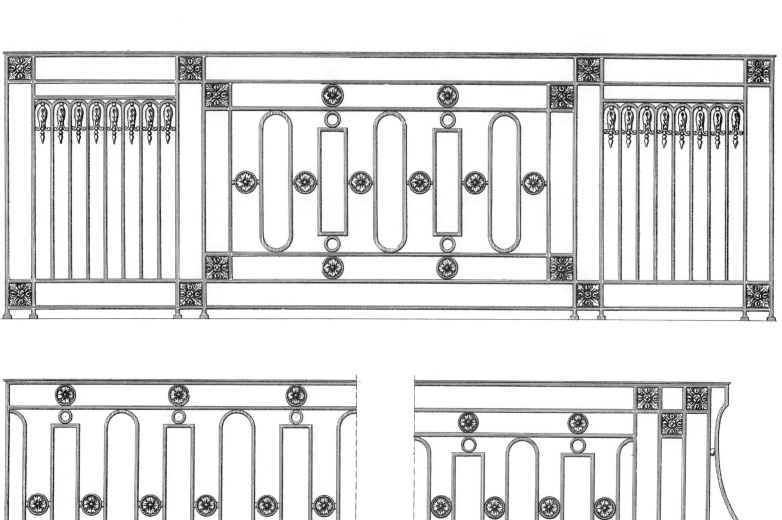

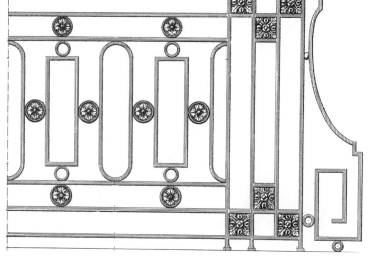

Plate 35. Large Balconies and Railings

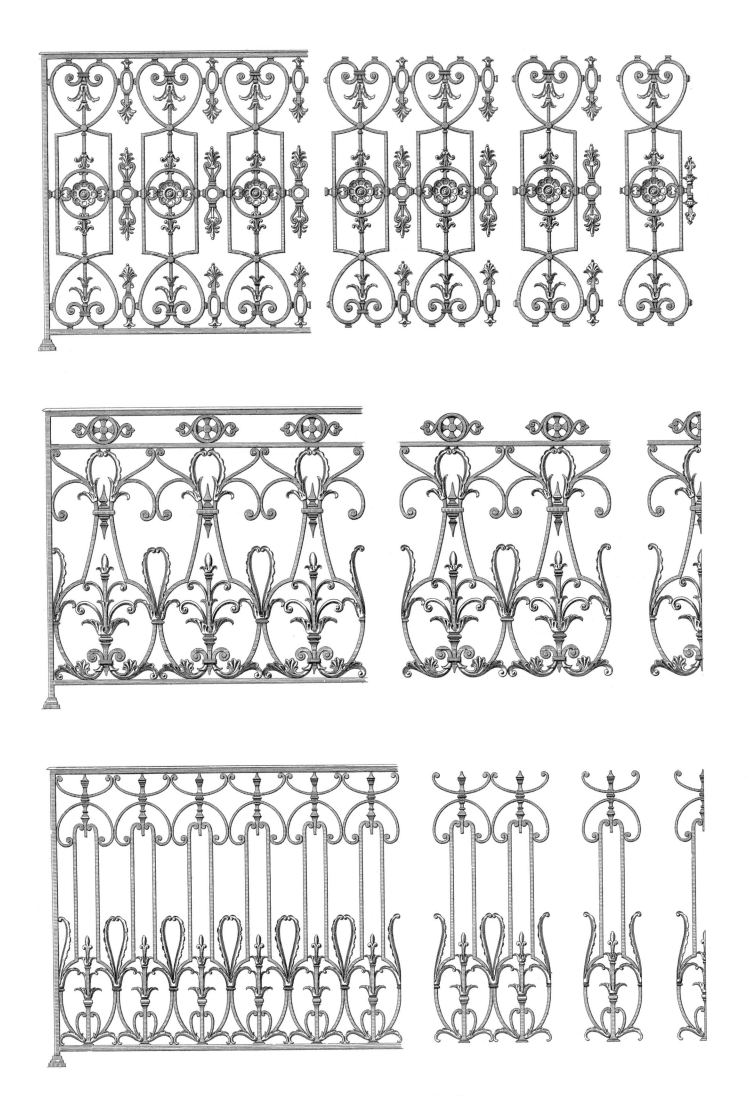

Plate 36. Large Balconies and Railings

Plate 37. Large Balconies and Railings

Plate 38. Large Balconies and Railings

Plate 39. Projecting Balconies

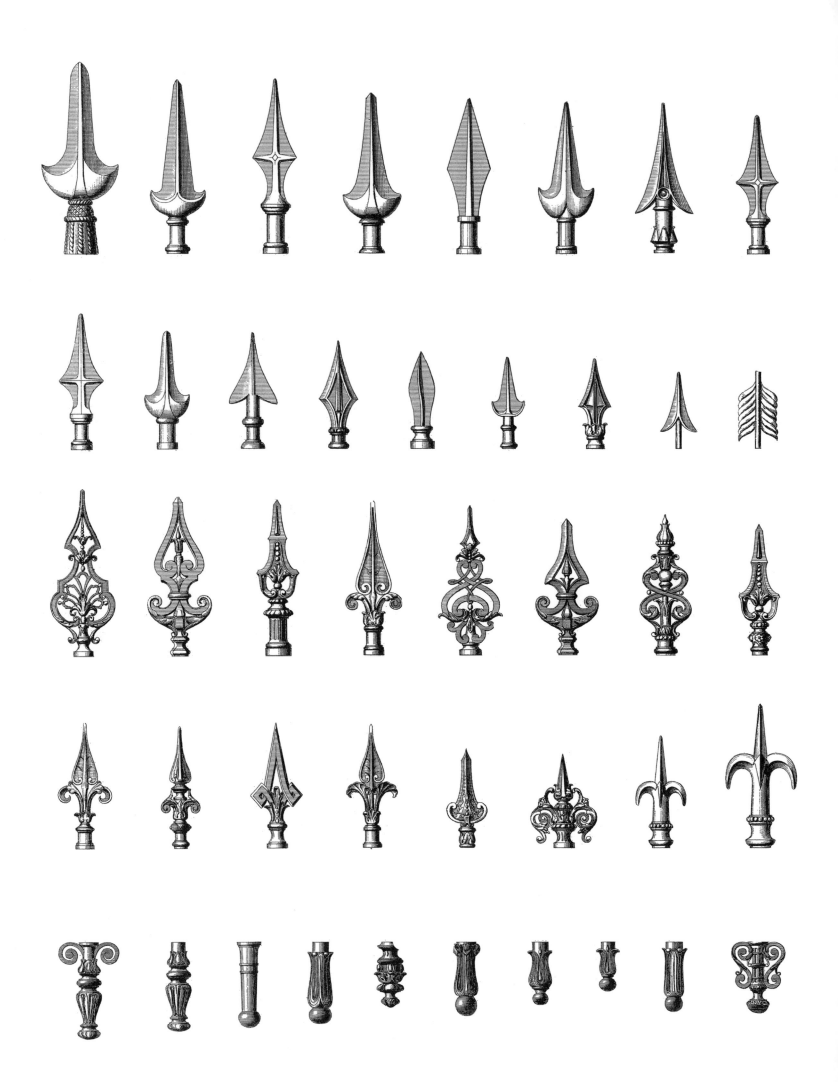

Plate 40. Railing Ornaments

Plate 41. Railing Ornaments

Plate 42. Railing Ornaments

Plate 43. Railing Ornaments

Plate 44. Railing Ornaments and Sections

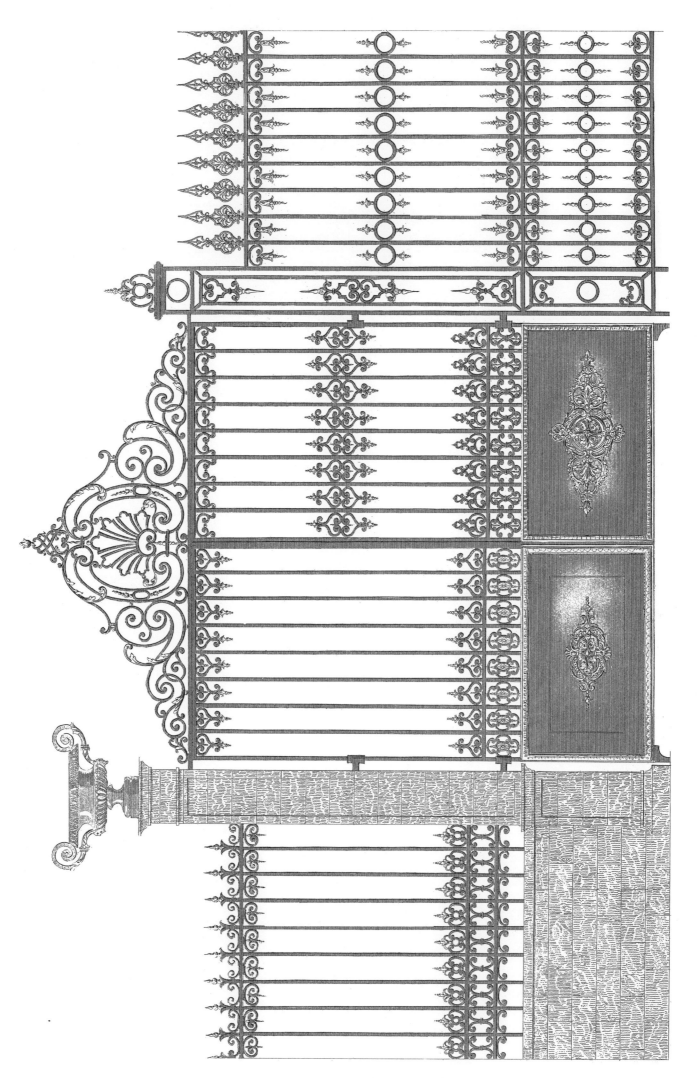

Plate 45. Railing Sections with Gate

Plate 46. Louis XV-Style Gate

Plate 47. Fanlight, Panels, and Transoms

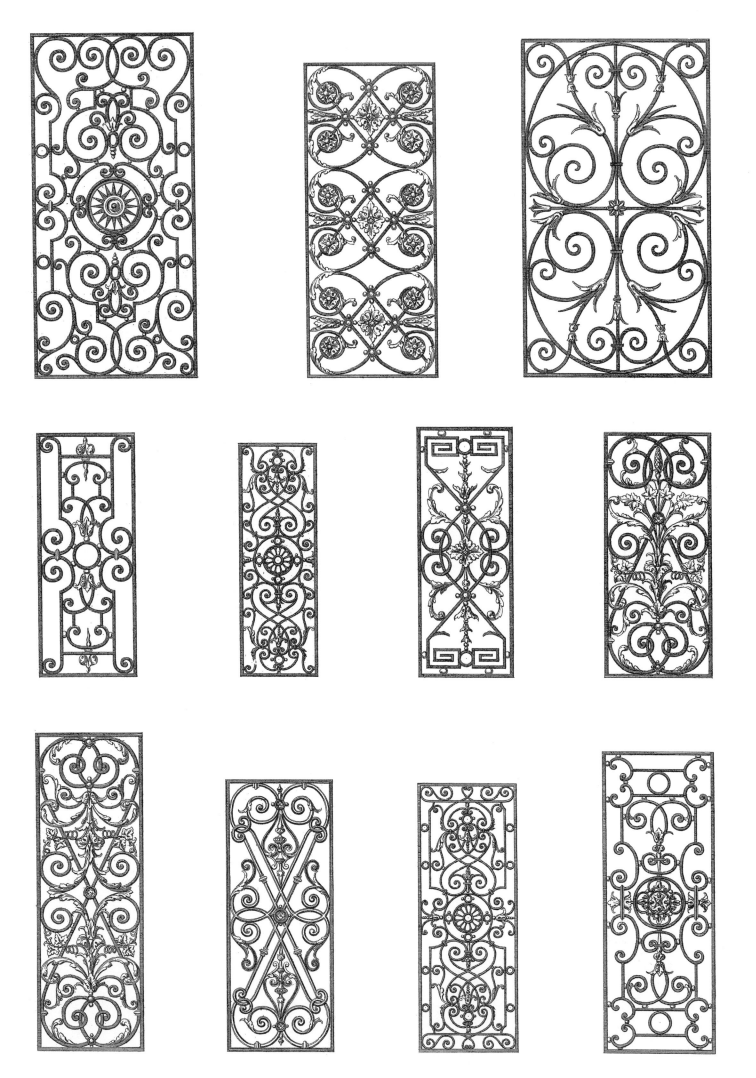

Plate 48. Door Panels and Transoms

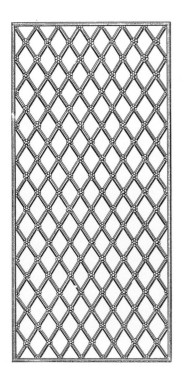
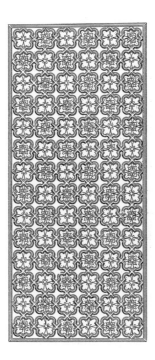
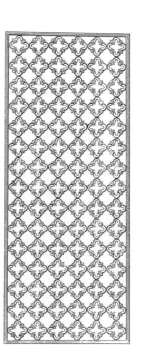

Plate 49. Door Panels and Transoms

Plate 50. Door Panels and Transoms

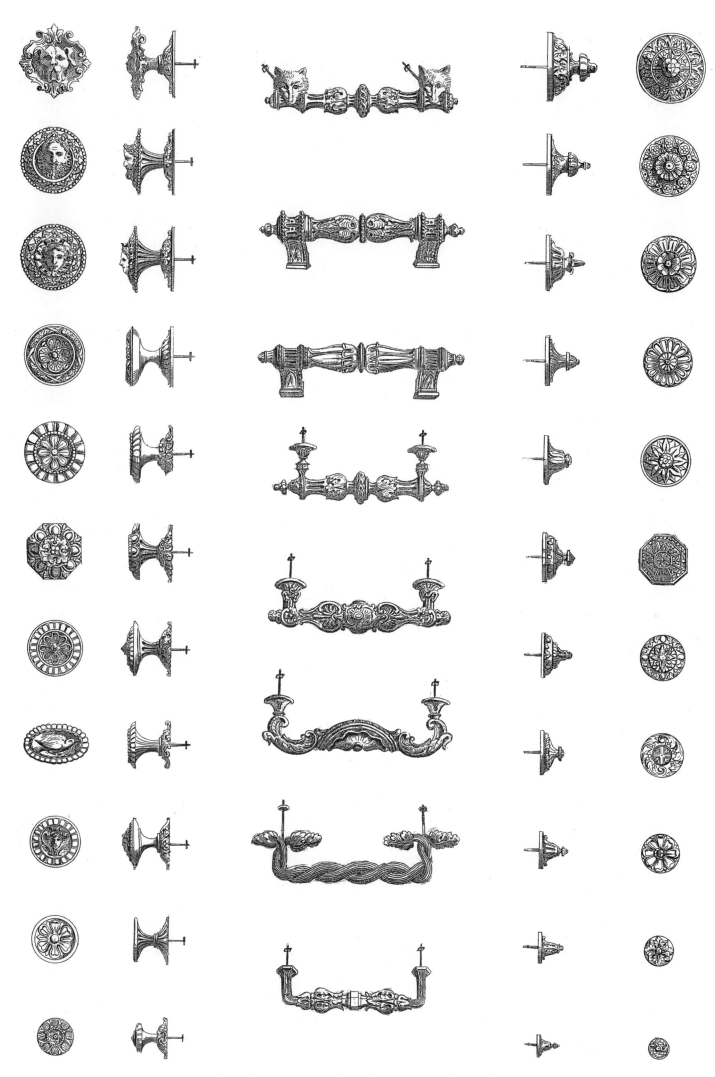

Plate 51. Doorknobs, Door Handles, and Doornails

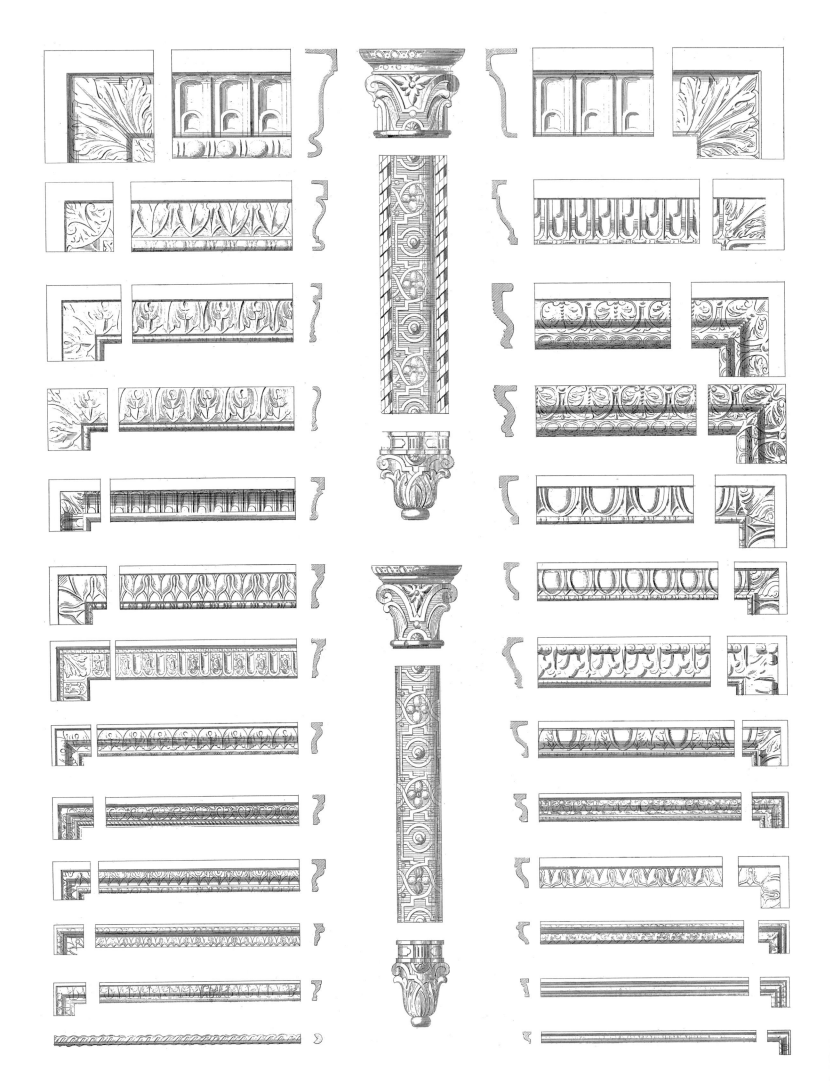

Plate 52. Moldings and Dividers

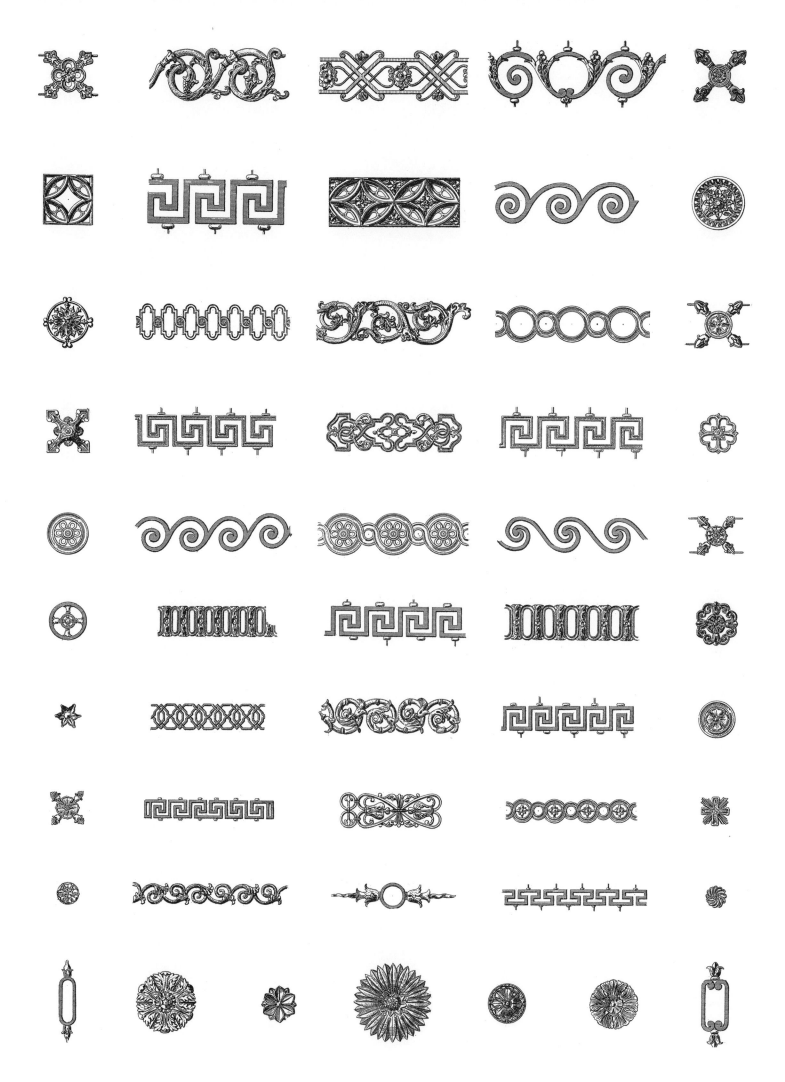

Plate 53. Friezes, Corner Crosses and Rosettes

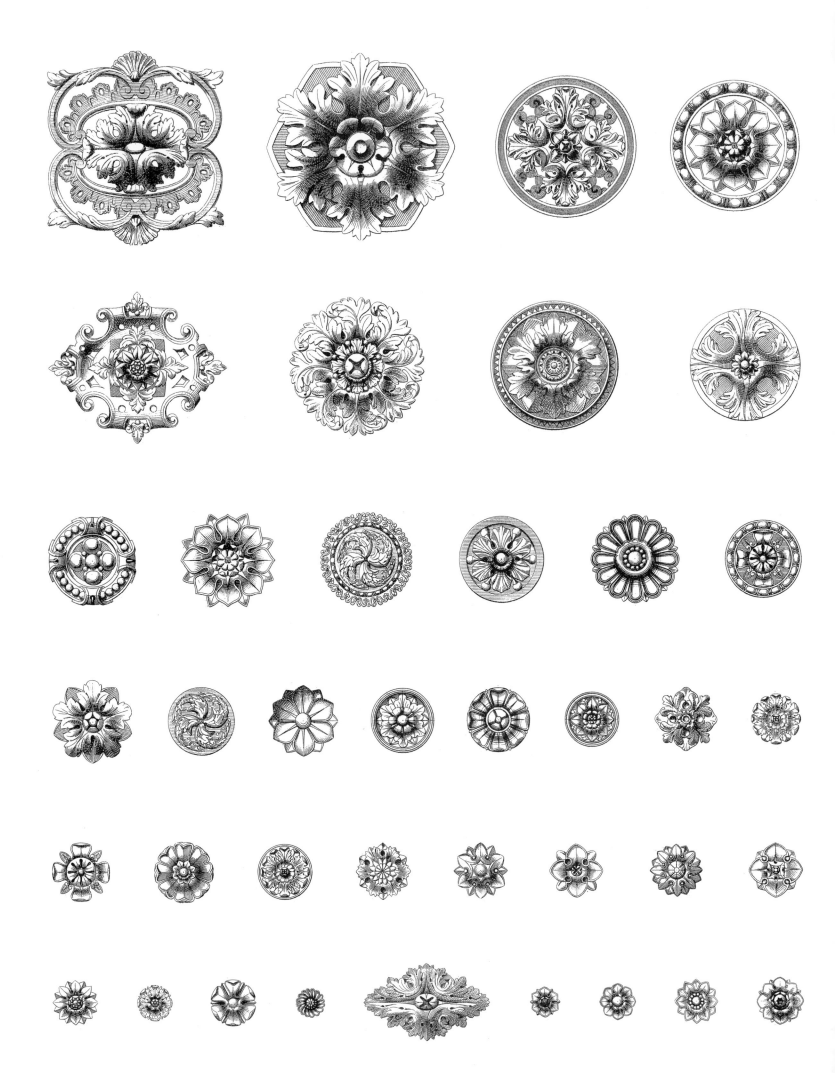

Plate 54. Detached Rosettes

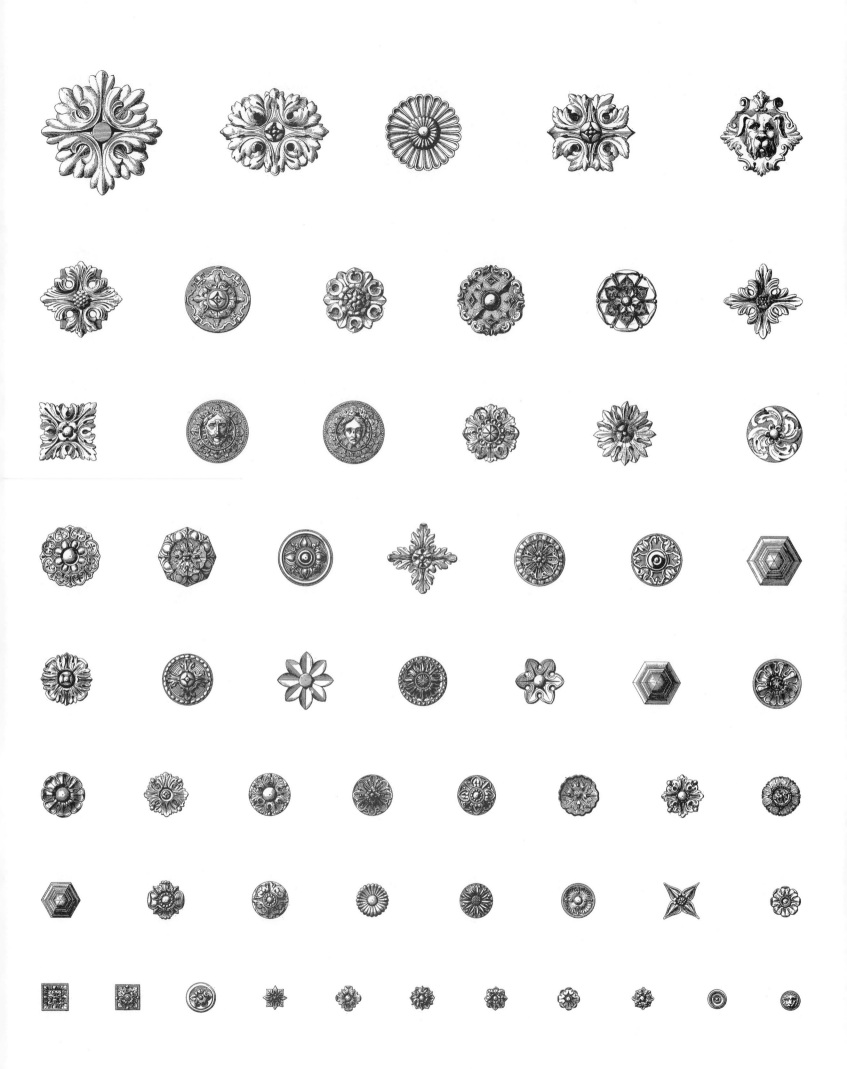

Plate 55. Detached Rosettes

Plate 56. Various Gargoyles and Heads

Plate 57. Crown or Capping, Brackets, Shelf Supports

Plate 58. Crown Molding and Crown or Capping

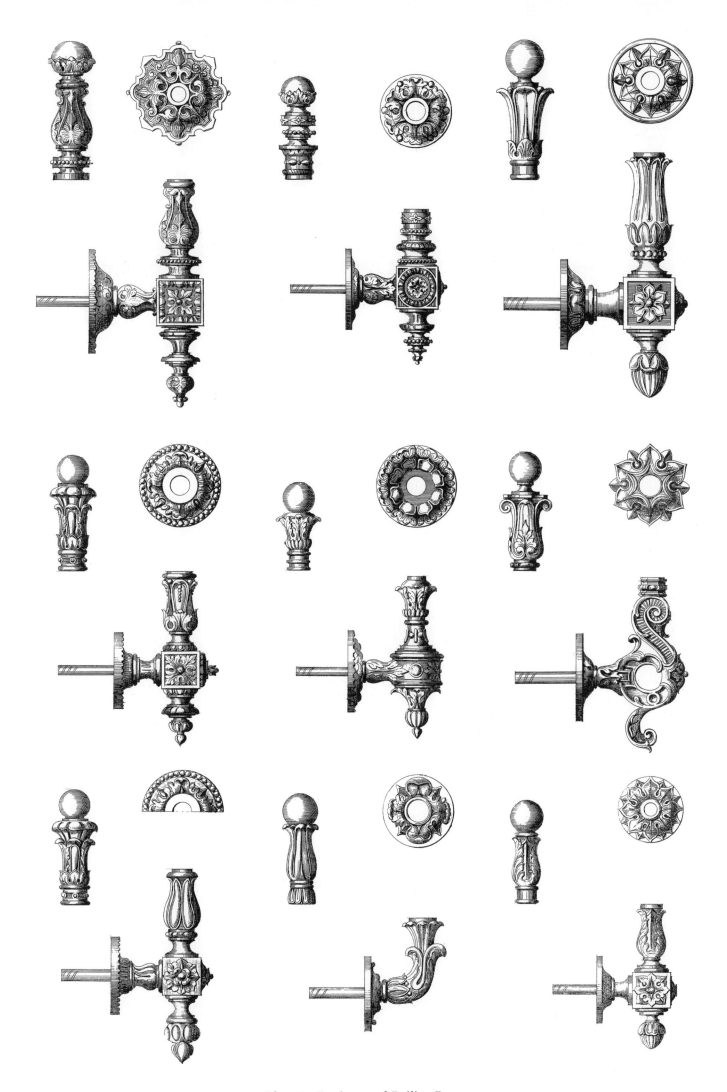

Plate 59. Banister and Railing Posts

Plate 60. Banister Trim

Plate 61. Banister Trim

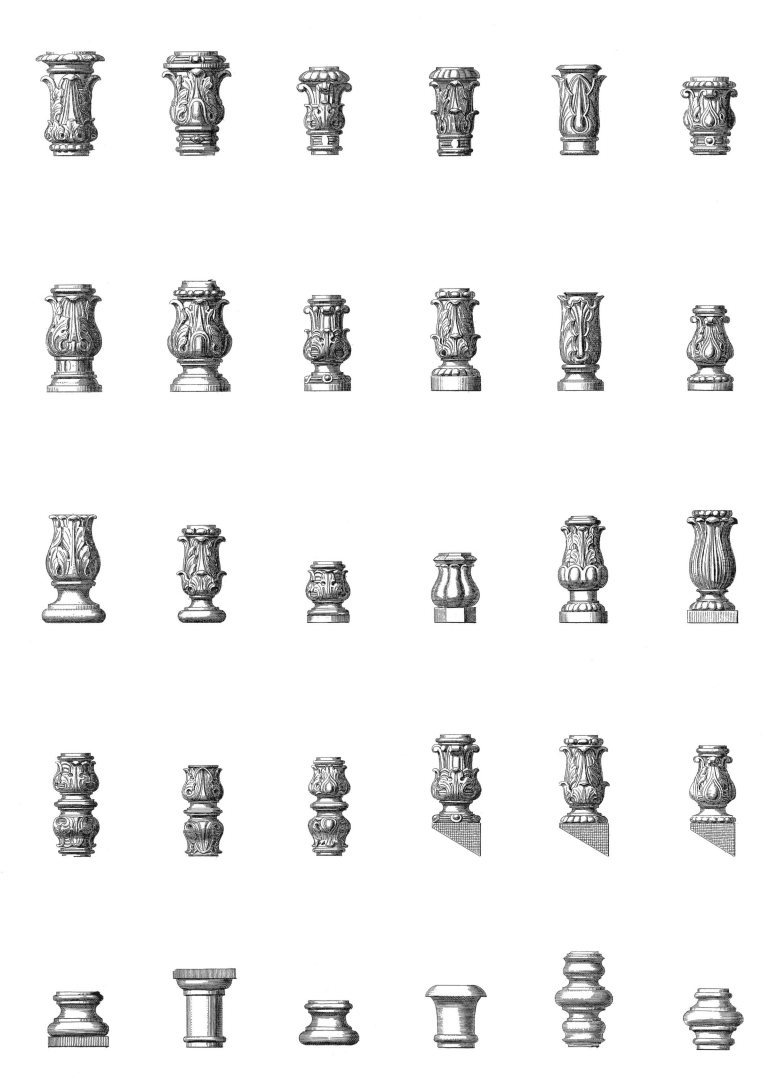

Plate 62. Banister Trim

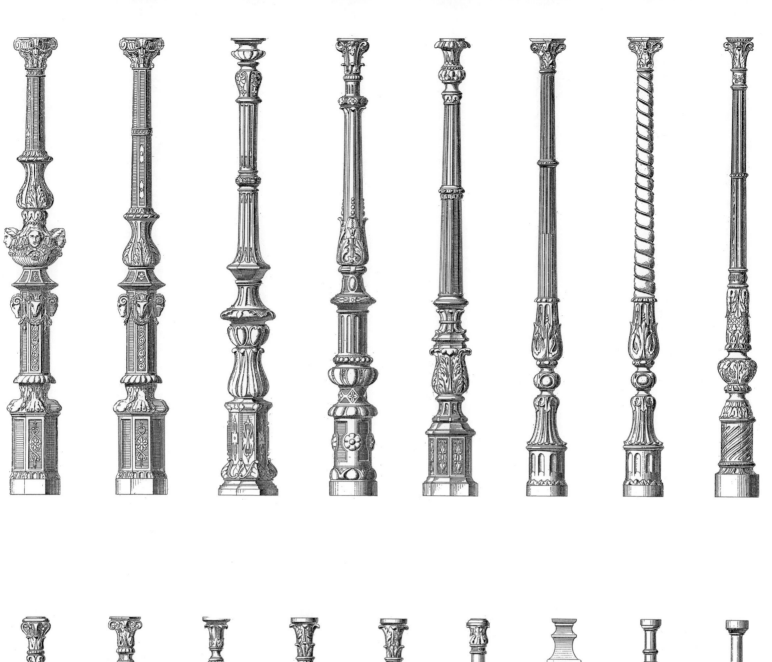

Plate 63. Hollow Trim

Plate 64. Banister Knobs

Plate 65. Table Bases, Shoe Scrapers, and Clotheshorses

Plate 66. Umbrella Racks

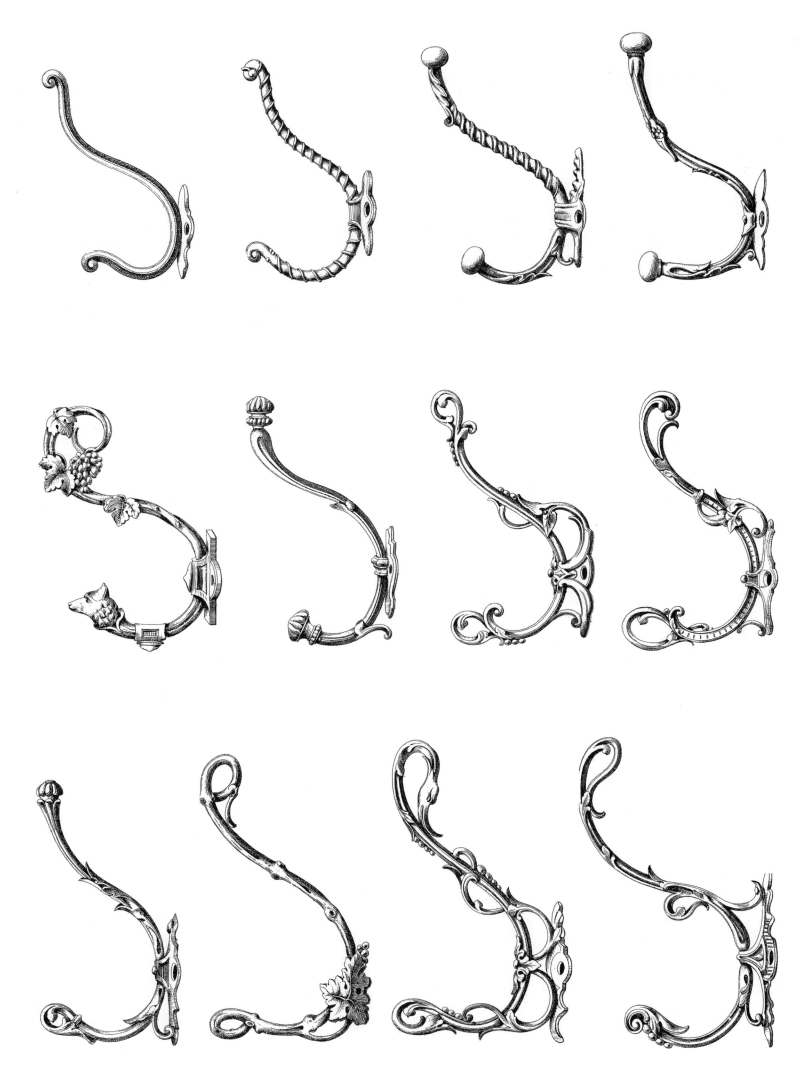

Plate 67. Hat Hooks

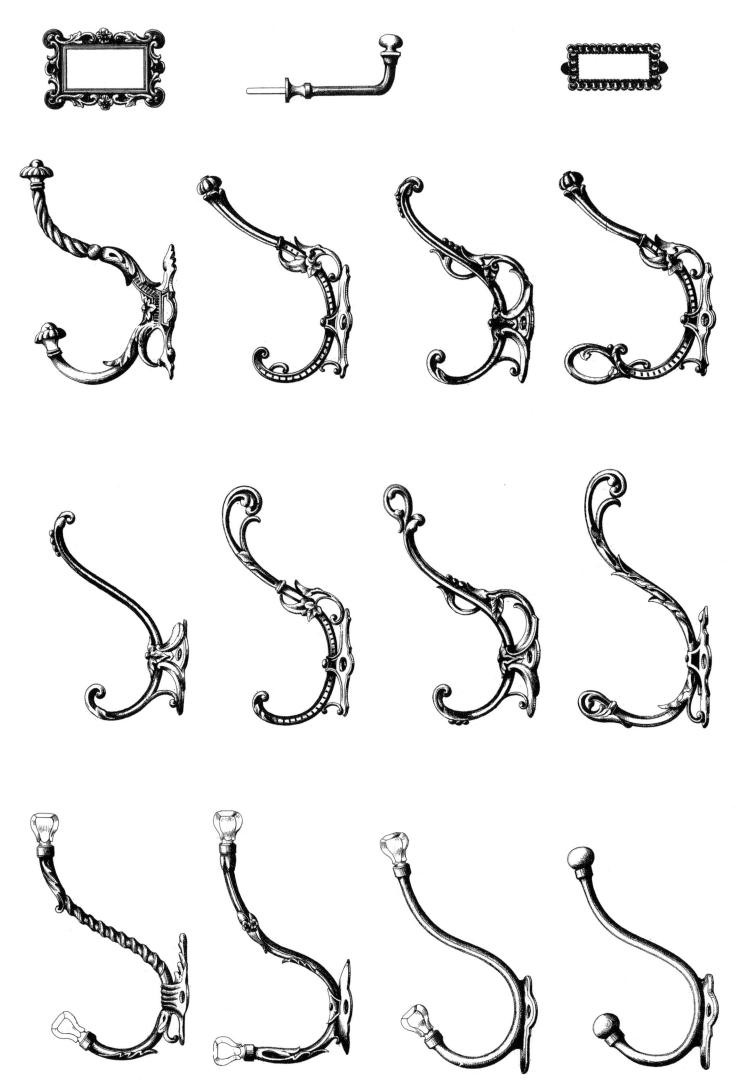

Plate 68. Hat Hooks

Plate 69. Racks for Fireplace Shovel and Tongs

Plate 70. Garden Bench Frames, Urns, and Vases

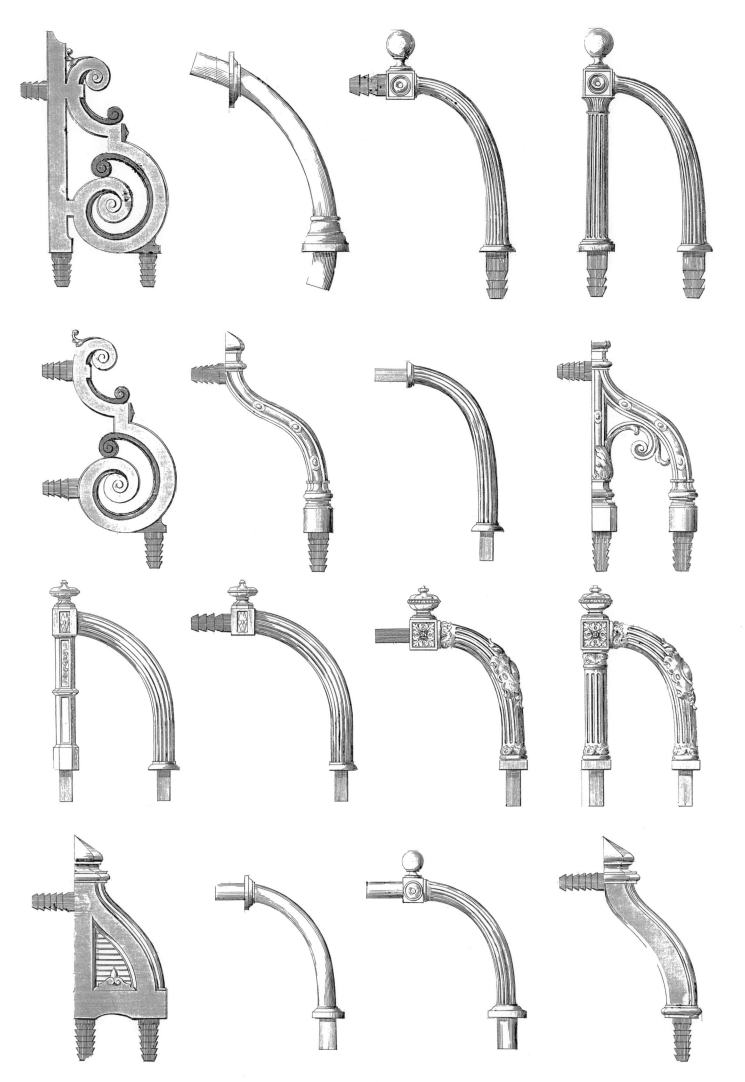

Plate 71. Collision Guards for Exterior Walls

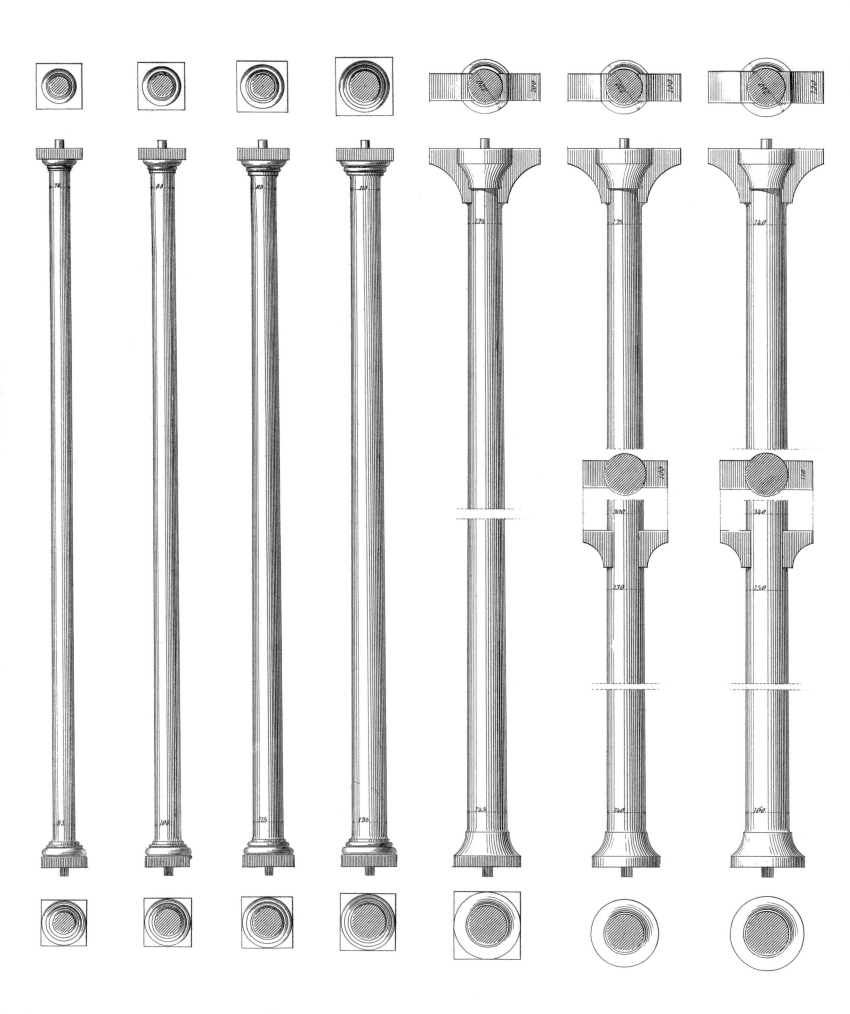

Plate 72. Full Columns

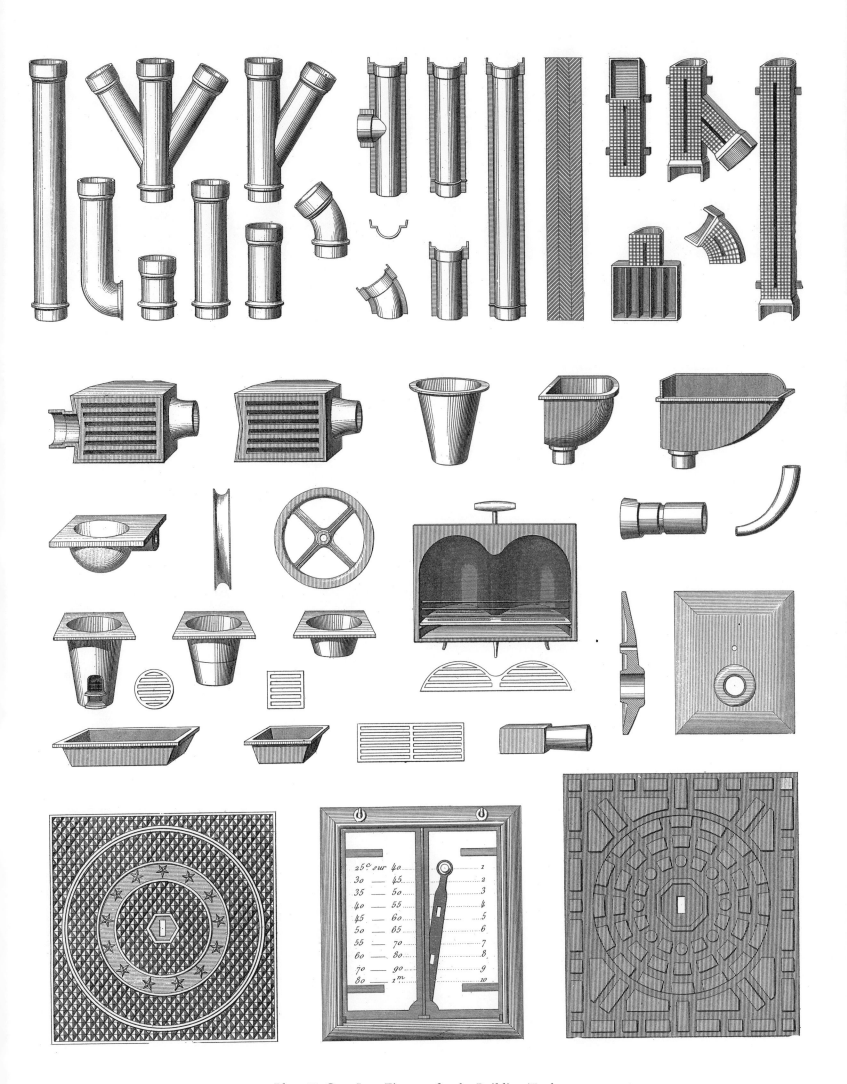

Plate 73. Cast-Iron Fixtures for the Building Trade

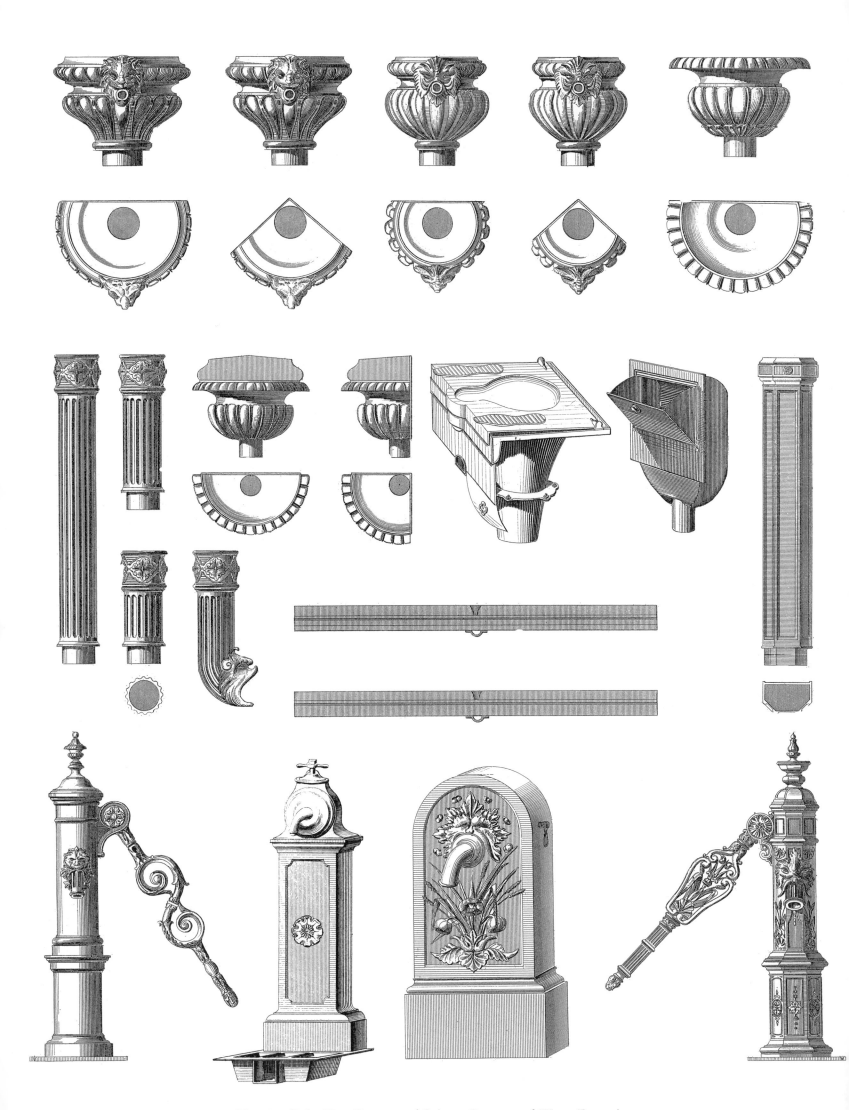

Plate 74. Sinks, Pipe Faucets and Spigots, Pumps, and Water Fountains

Plate 75. Candleholders

Plate 76. Religious Statues

Plate 77. Crosses

Plate 78. Crosses

Plate 79. Crosses

Plate 80. Crosses

Plate 81. Crosses

Plate 82. Crosses

Plate 83. Crosses

Plate 84. Tomb Enclosures

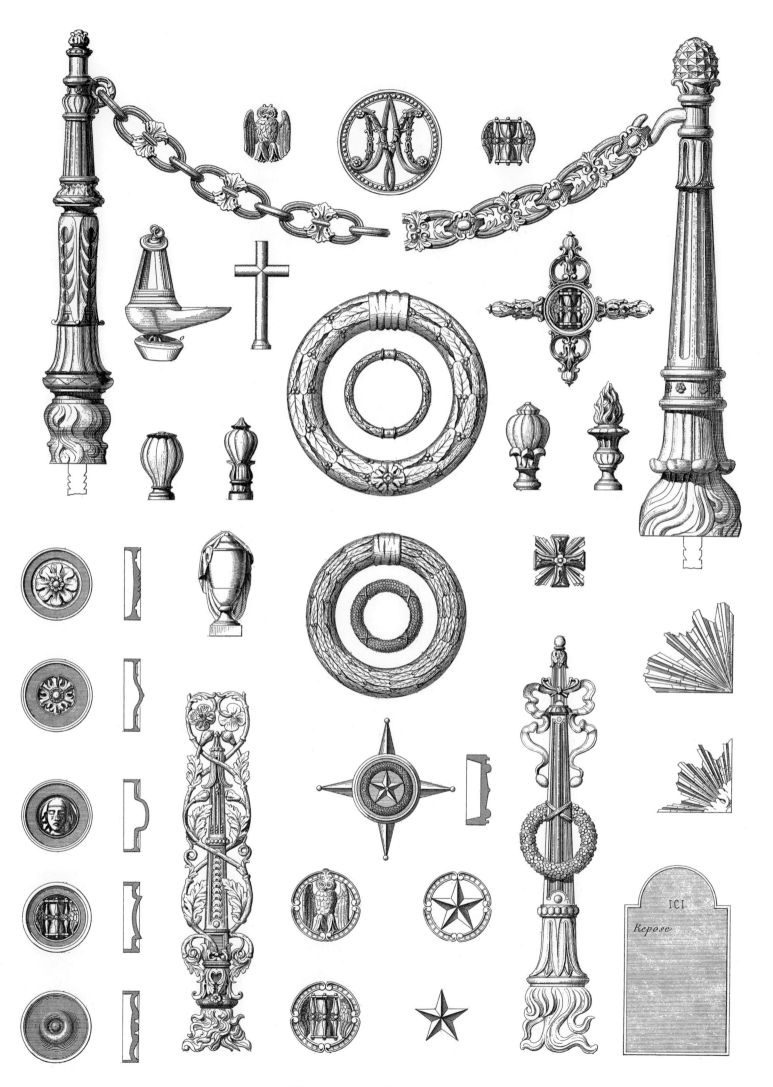

Plate 85. Funeral Ornaments

Plate 86. Funeral Monuments